THIS COLORING BOOK
BELONGS TO:

- - - - - - - - - - - - - - - - - - - -

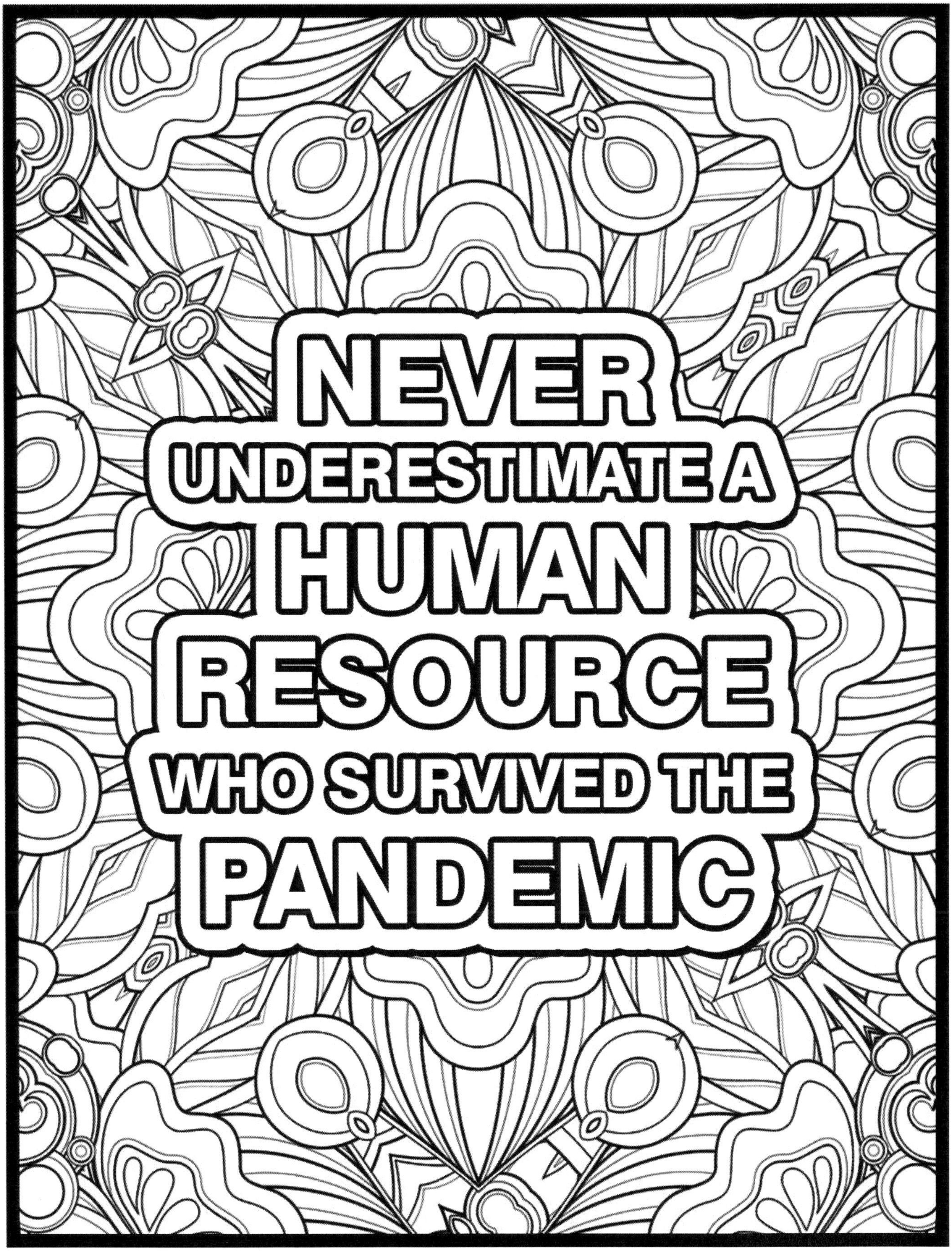
NEVER
UNDERESTIMATE A
HUMAN
RESOURCE
WHO SURVIVED THE
PANDEMIC

OTHER
HUMAN
RESOURCES
Me

INSTANT
HUMAN
RESOURCES
JUST ADD
COFFEE

I'm in
Human Resources
What's your
Fucking
SuperPower?

HR
llama
ain't got time
for your drama

This day was such as a
Clusterfuck
and i don't give a
Shit!

DON'T MAKE
ME USE MY
HUMAN RESOURCES
Voice

STFU!
JUST ASSUME
I'M
Always
RIGHT!

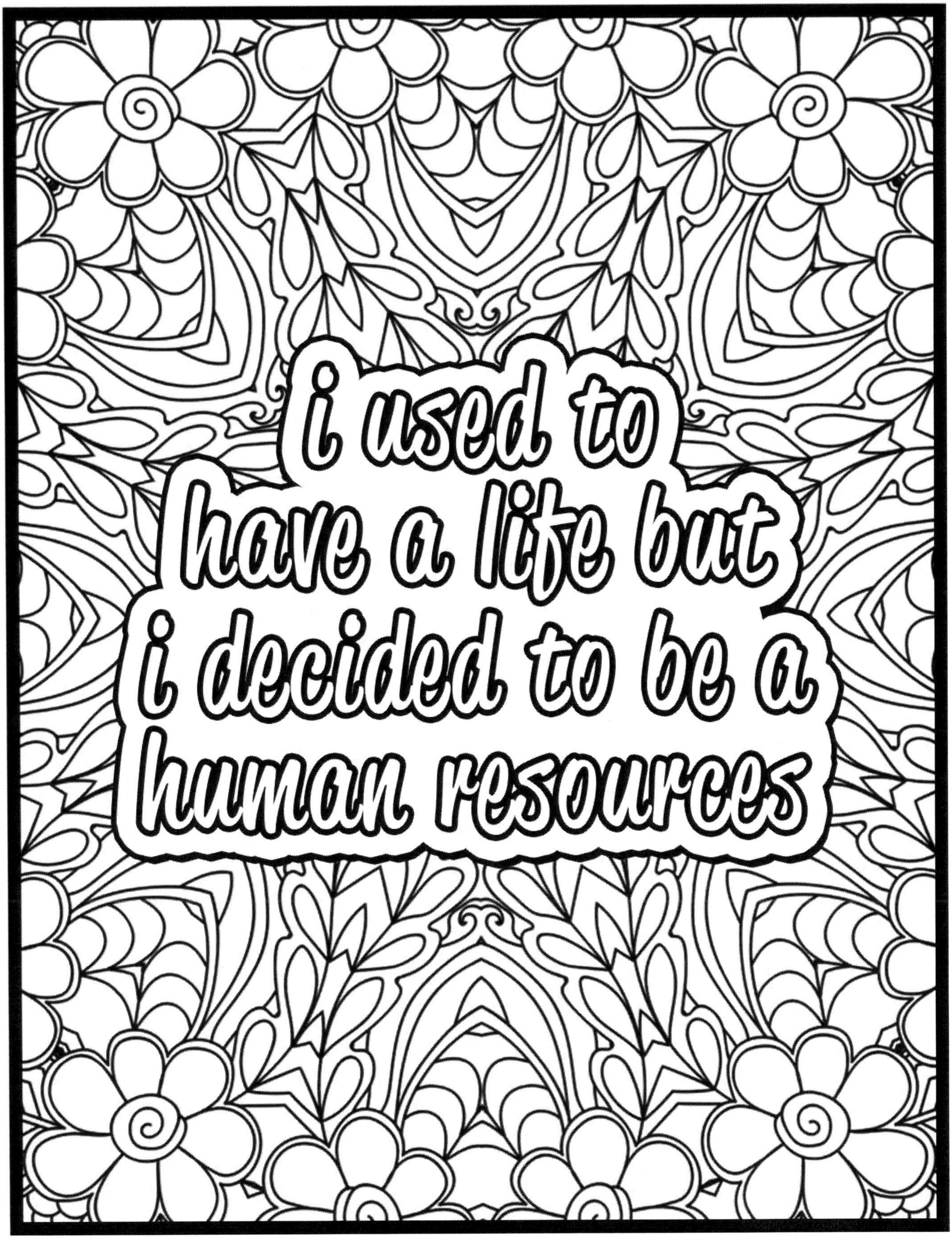
i used to
have a life but
i decided to be a
human resources

THIS
HR
IS OFF
DUTY

FUCKING
LEGEND

49%
Human
resources
51%
BADASS

ESSENTIAL
AF

IT'S A
HR
THING
YOU'D NOT
UNDERSTAND

I'VE GOT
99
PROBLEMS
BUT
COLORING
AIN'T ONE

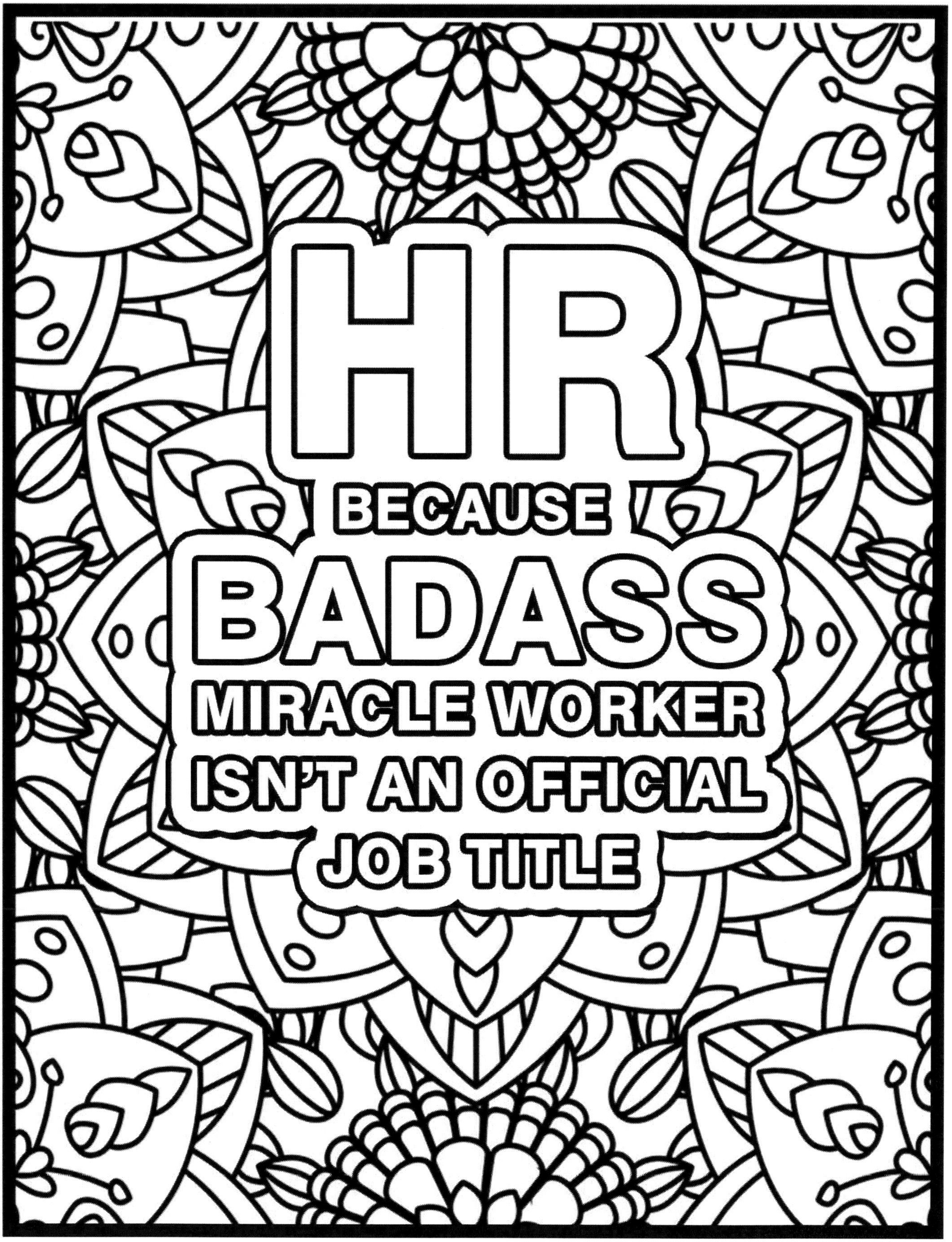
HR
BECAUSE
BADASS
MIRACLE WORKER
ISN'T AN OFFICIAL
JOB TITLE

this
Human
Resource
needs a
Mother
Fucking
Drink

SORRY
I'M DONE
HELPING
ASSHOLES
TODAY

World's
Okayest
Human
Resource

Made in United States
North Haven, CT
08 May 2022

19011663R00026